Reflection of the Light

Irwin J. Goldman

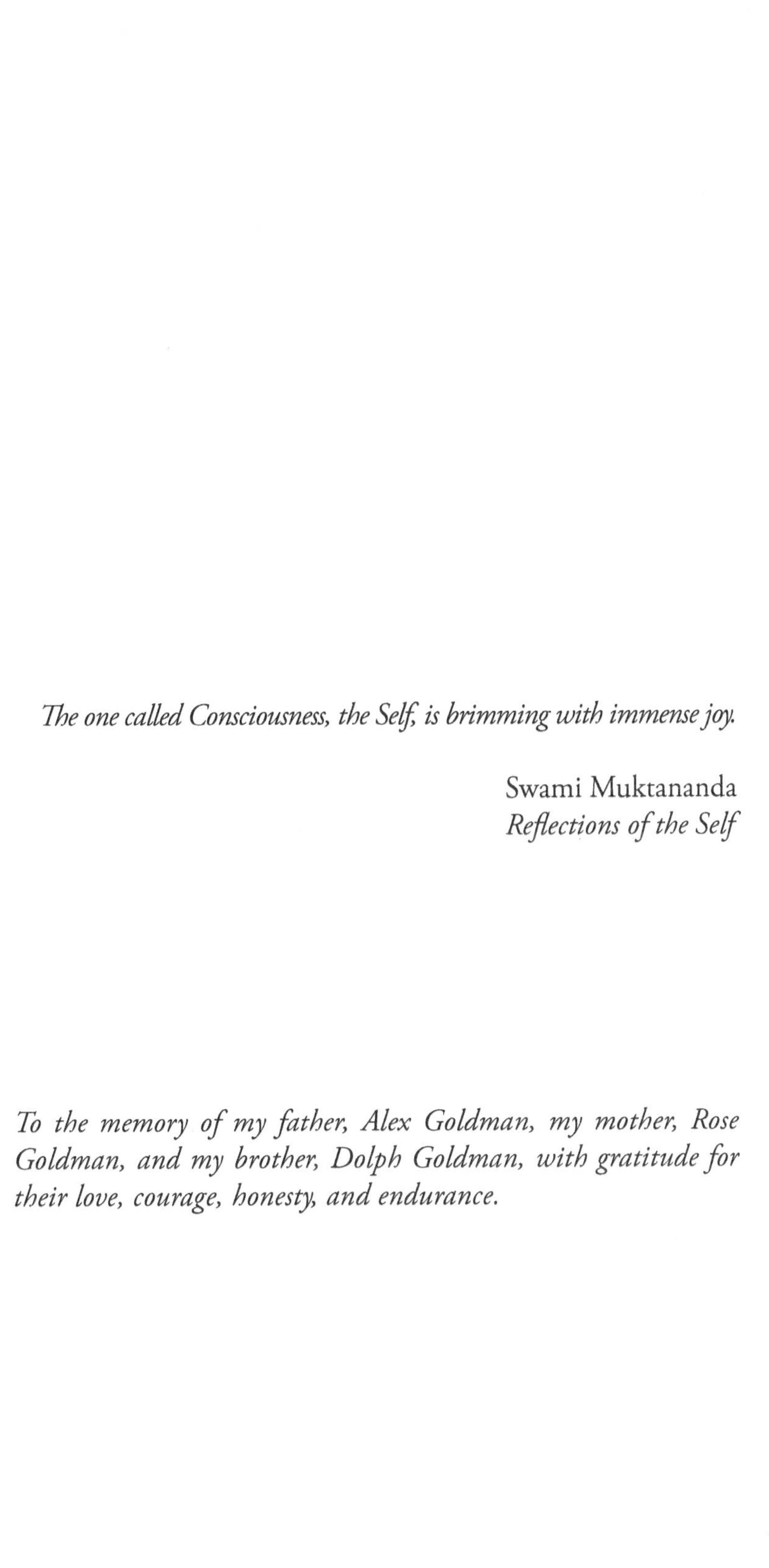

The one called Consciousness, the Self, is brimming with immense joy.

Swami Muktananda
Reflections of the Self

To the memory of my father, Alex Goldman, my mother, Rose Goldman, and my brother, Dolph Goldman, with gratitude for their love, courage, honesty, and endurance.

Reflection of the Light
by Irwin J. Goldman

ISBN: 9798554647727
Library of Congress: 2020921906

Dunton Publishing
New York, New York
duntonpublishing.com

To The Reader

I wrote these poems in the eighth decade of my life in a poetry workshop originated by Michelle de Savigny at the Hamilton Senior Center in New York City and presently guided by Chocolate Waters. They reflect salient thoughts, feelings, experiences, reflections and perspectives of this period of my life and, for me, are a self-portrait in poetry.

Two new friends appear in many of these poems. I met one, Ebru, when she moved into the apartment directly below my own. Newly married, new to this country, and learning to cook, Ebru took a liking to her upstairs neighbor and decided to share some of the results of her cooking skills with him. The Ebru poems are a result of that decision.

The second friend, Anita, is a Christian Science practitioner whose profound spiritual understanding appeared to me similar to that more prominently found in Eastern philosophy. In my poems she has become a seer and yogini. The poems are a mixture of actuality and imagination.

I hope the reader will enjoy the poems and be stimulated by them. The outlook presented in the Anita poems and in others is carefully examined by Aldous Huxley in his book *The Perennial Philosophy* and a Christian formulation appears in Mary Baker Eddy's *Science and Health with Key to the Scriptures*.

The poems are best read from first to last as those later in the book often depend on earlier ones for their clarity and effect.

Table of Contents

Teacher of Poetry

The human headlong race stops for me
When I see
Our teacher
Envelop her flock of poets
With her loving attention
(I think unknowingly—
It is her nature.)

I remember then what Plato taught:
True learning comes direct,
One person to one person,
Eye to eye,
Smile to smile,
For what you teach is what you are.

A Morning Conversation

Anita was serving tea on a small balcony.
It's now or never, she told me,
If you want heaven and seek it,
Your seeking is forever—
Because it's now or never.

If I see a woman praying silently
In a church, I asked, or a man
Kneeling before a sacred image,
Or folks fasting on a holy day,
Are you saying they will never reach heaven?
Those are harsh words from you, Anita.

Not at all, she answered,
What is unreachable is right where you are.
There's nowhere to go if you're already there.

Tell me, Anita,
When you fell on ice last winter
And fractured the vertebrae of your spine,
You walked like an automaton
With a silent grunt at every step.
Were you in heaven then?
It doesn't seem believable.

Friend. Her voice was gentle.
Your eyes saw a body in agony
And imagined a mouth with a silent cry.
But with every step I took
I was saying: God is my structure,

God is my substance, my joy, my life.
My mind was not where you were looking.

All right, I countered, the question of questions, then—
Did an all-loving God cause that accident to you?
Those fractures in your vertebrae?
What is your answer to that?

Anita glanced to the sky and said softly,
What accident?
What fractures? What vertebrae?
Look! There's a hawk circling above us.
It's such a beautiful morning.

Ebru's Cake

When Ebru bakes a cake,
She puts in chocolate,
Sunshine, coconut flakes and love
And brings it to your door.
You hear a gentle voice,
"It's Ebru."
And there she stands before you, happily,
Holding out a portion of her genius.
My mother never baked a cake.
But somehow, next morning
I feel her presence behind me,
Closely watching,
As I drink my chamomile tea
And Ebru's cake slowly
Vanishes into my body.

A Fair Exchange

Thank God, I say,
The expensive pearl was
Outside my reach—
The pearl without price
Fell into my hand.

Your Chuckle

For A.K.

Your chuckle is as welcoming
As my peach tree, embracing
Its unexpected visitors from Paris or Rome,
Bold sparrow stowaways on boats of freight
Now in the parks and streets of New York.
You can tell them by their beaks,
Not for pecking but for cracking,
And with their chubby, healthy look
They seem to chuckle too.
I watch these winter travelers from my window
As they hop from branch to branch,
Look about cheerily, silently,
And suddenly fly off, entrusting me
With their message: that there is a lightness
To the universe, a buoyancy to all its constellations
And the final sound at the end of time
May well resemble
Your chuckle.

Mindfulness

Fear has settled over me,
It dries my throat,
Stops my voice,
Digs a home beneath my heart;
It grows stronger, gobbling down my every thought.
And yet, it cannot abide the power
Of a pure gaze.

No Longer So: A Bird in the Hand

I wouldn't know
What to do
With a bird in my hand,
Each of us
In fear and distress.
But two birds in the bush can
Delight my eyes,
Call forth a smile,
Teach me anew about
The joy of life.

Only Love

Only love is happening,
Anita tells me,
No sunless days, no broken bones,
No feelings hurt—
Only peace is happening, she says.

The railway tracks belie the 20-20 eye.
They never meet some place far off.
The trains go safe,
The riders are content.

Your body shines forth in glory you won't see
Until you know the truth, she says,
Until you know that only love is happening—
And nothing else.

Birds in the City

The sparrows peck at the hot cement
And with heads bobbing to their own beat
The pigeons rush forward, flap wings, fly and return
While I watch through a large window,
Holding a cool drink.
What can the walls of buildings mean,
The assault of fume and noise,
To creatures with wings and melody?
They serve us:
Give us pleasure at their sight—
Remind us we are free beings.
They'd rather be near streams and fields,
With the whole sky visible in a glance.
But here they are, and here they stay, for a day,
                    a year, a lifetime.

A Moment

What comes when it goes
And goes when it comes?
As elusive as memory.
We give it a name—
We make it seem real.

Ebru's Soup

Better than a therapist,
Better than a session of yoga,
Ebru's Turkish yellow-lentil soup
Will bring a smile to all parts
Of your body. People will ask,
"Did you win the lottery?"
"Were you on vacation?"
It's her mother's ancient recipe
And a modern electric blender
That works the magic.
Or, perhaps the poet Rumi in ecstasy
Inhabiting her pots—
One who sang of God's joy
Even in soup.

A Question of Life and Death

What do you think of philosophers, I asked Anita,
While she was arranging carnations
In a translucent vase.
An interesting group, she replied,
Consider Mister A.J. Ayers,
The most important philosopher in England,
A fierce debater—
Insisted life ended with the physical,
No soul, no deity, no
Wishful thinking for *him*—
Knighted by the queen. But see
What happened
In his first dying, so to speak.

Lying one night in a hospital bed,
Struggling with the germs of pneumonia,
One of his old girlfriends came to visit him
With an appealing slice of salmon,
And while the nurses were looking elsewhere,
She slipped it to him—
But he choked on it, gasped
And found himself—
In heaven!
A place he didn't believe in
Or ever expect to see,
A place of color and wonder,
With guardian spirits in the form of light,
Instructing him on the ways of the astral world
And a Divine Being in their midst!

But while he was learning to communicate
With his heavenly guides, his earthly doctors
Were beating on his chest,
And in four minutes his heart revived,
With beeping and commotion around him
And a frightened girlfriend looking on.

So did he change his thinking, I asked Anita.
In no way, was her response.
At first he told his doctor
He would have to revise
All his ideas and books,
But after consulting with friends, family,
And fellow philosophers,
He concluded his mind had played
A trick on him,
What with the drugs, the stress
And the smoked salmon—
And his experience of heaven, he decided,
Was nothing but a fantasia of the mind.

And what do you take from all this, I then asked.
Anita held up the vase of flowers
For me to gaze on.
Pink, red and white carnations
Gazed back.

From the beauty they have seen, she replied,
There are those who trust
In a beauty they have yet to see.
When they enter heaven, they say,
I know this place.
I've been here already.
I never left it.
Listen to such as these
And learn from them all.

Miracle

There I am, here, now.
Did not order it, did not request it.
And so every table, twig, and hair
Of every head,
Every boulder and pebble—
Coming out of its silence
To whirl in the universe for a spell
As I do here, now.

Vantage Point

Looking forward, freedom.
Looking backward, destiny.
What I am, I am—
No other would I wish to be.

Touch of the Masters

What can compare to the touch of the masters?
The strong gentle hands of Muktananda
Awaited in silence, in deep meditation.
The soft embrace, once, then again, then a third time
Of Ammaji the Mother,
She cannot help but hug her children.
They can touch with a look:
Mother Meera gazes deeply into the eyes,
And Nityanada's look could stop a train.
In this way they bless a sorrowing world
And open the way to a forgotten truth.

Saundra

Her ashes are buried
On a hill that overlooks
The Croatian village of Medjugorje.
Here, the mother of Jesus appeared
To six village children and here
My friend felt most at home.
She was an actress who loved to speak.
No words are needed now:
She is with me whenever I wish to know
She is with me. Her silent presence
Tells me all.

Anita on My Birthday

It's my birthday, I told Anita,
Wish me a happy birthday.

It isn't your birthday, she replied,
You were never born, will never die
And you do not have a birthday!

Eighty-three years ago wasn't I
Pushed out,
Ejected from my mother's struggling body—
Are you denying that?

I am, she said,
That baby is a floating dream
In a mind not even yours.
As real as last winter's snowflake
In tomorrow's backyard.

Wish me a happy birthday anyway,
I pressed my friend.

I wish you happy eternity, was her answer.
And if you choose to be a prisoner of time,
A happy birthday as well.

The Celestial Bells

…to the moaning and the groaning of the bells.
Edgar Allen Poe

Hear the great celestial bells, ethereal bells—
What a world of woe their symphony dispels!
In the clear, crisp air of dawn
We arise, surprised, newborn,
As our thoughts go whirling round
Reverberating with the sound
Of *Om*—
The powerful sound of *Om*
From the bells, from the bells,
From the bells;
Enraptured by the joyful bells
We sense a truth beyond our dreams—
The love that *is*,
The play that *seems*
And vanishes as we travel home
To the ringing of the bells,
Of the bells—
To their singing and their soaring,
To the light-in-us restoring
To the gladness and the glory of the bells.

Sparkles of the Day

God came to me in the form of Dennis
Calling to say he was cooking zucchini
And spaghetti—all in one pot—
With two inches of water,
The spaghetti very thin.
And how he saw this book on Tennessee Williams
With many photos, at B and N,
And once at a bar on Broadway
Tennessee came by, but Dennis didn't call to him,
God is so casual.
I told Dennis I've never cooked zucchini
And he should write a book about saving water.
He said, 'see ya buddy' and I, 'take care, Dennis'
But it was *namaste* I was hearing all the time.

The Voice

It was Linda calling,
A bright, upbeat voice,
So glad she got *me*,
Not the message machine.
So glad I was eligible
For an *amazing* Caribbean cruise.
I shouted into the phone,
"Is this a person or a machine?"
The voice ignored my question,
Eager to instruct me
How to obtain my fantastic cruise.
I hung up in midsentence
To show my displeasure
All the while knowing a Linda-less voice
Existed in its own dimension,
Unmoved by the dilemmas of mortals
Or our discontents.

Ebru in the Kitchen

When Ebru prepares a meal
It's a ballet—
She pirouettes in all directions,
Twirls and bends,
Because there's a stove and a fridge,
Cupboards and a sink,
All to consider in the same moment.
One hand stirs the pot,
One hand washes the lettuce,
One hand takes out the yogurt,
One hand pulls up a sauce pan—
It's Brahma in the dance of creation!
Never mind the Taj Mahal
Or the stones of Stonehenge,
Ebru in her kitchen is
Wonder enough.

The Self You Cannot See

The self you cannot see is more interesting
Than the self you can, Anita says.
When winter snow glimmers in morning sunlight
You may sense it.
A poet came upon it when he heard
The singing of a lark.
He longed to know the secret of such gladness.

A curious wish, says Anita,
Since he, himself, is what he seeks.
If he could know his own splendor,
His eyes would clear, his art would sing.

A Dental Appointment

I am come in the guise of
He-whose-tooth-needs-repair.
In this manner I bring glory to you,
As you to me.
I wear a shirt of many colors,
You are dressed in white.
You bow to me and I bow to you,
Two singular drops from a vast sea of light.
With this symmetry we bring to the great cosmos
Just what it needs
At the perfect time and place.

Knowing

If you place a mirror before a mirror
And in one mirror
You see the other
And in the mirror within the mirror
You see the first again
And on and on into infinity
Or you peer into the contorting mirrors
In the funhouse of an amusement park
In one your body is squashed down
In the other stretched out
You may begin to question
When you look into the face
Of your dearest friend
Am I seeing a reflection
Of a reflection
Am I seeing a contortion
Or a distortion
You may but you never will
Because you know what you know
And you know that you know
What you know—which is
How beautiful is this face
How good it is to look upon
And your mind ceases
Its own reflections upon reflections
Contortions and distortions
Abides in what it knows
And what it is
And brings you at long last
To the point of rest.

Travels

The sparrows like my peach tree, it seems,
That little tree just outside my window.
Even on cold winter mornings they bless my sight.
They never stay long, jump from branch to branch
And fly away.

I think of them on their journey
To a place warmer than New York,
Building nests in the Carolina trees perhaps,
Or settling in the marshes and towns of Florida.

The geese of Central Park come from further north;
Their journeys are Odyssean I'm told.
New York is not the place for them and soon they're gone.

And I have traveled far at times,
Remember well the night train to Leningrad,
The road from Bombay to Ganeshpuri ashram,
The Adriatic coast, the Lake of Galilee.

Now my trips are inner ones,
The threshold is near that leads from this to that,
And I do muse on an unknown future:
Intimations from my dearest friend come to me,
Speaking of great tasks and great joy—
That is my hope and it lifts me high,
Sky-flying with the sparrows and the geese.

Anita Asks Me What I See

Anita asks me what I see
As I look upon the urban scene.
I speak of the gingko tree
Waiting for its leaves to grow,
The lamppost stretched four stories tall,
The passersby and the piled-up snow.

"All these things," she proffers a smile,
"In space arise and stay awhile
And then depart, and their counterpart
Is the space within…Oh, my friend,

Listen carefully—
The inner space is singer of your days.
It knows your every cry and fear,
It knows the manner of your ways,
The thoughts that come and disappear.
It is the dancer of your dance,
And when revealed, it brings the dawn,
But when concealed, your day is night;
To know it brings down the light—
For this purpose you were born."

I look within Anita's eyes—
My head's awhirl—
And then, surprise!
A sky-blue pearl is what I see—
Lustrous sign of what could be:
Clarity and mastery

In mystery.

In the Endgame

In the endgame of my earthly life
When my chess pieces
Had all but vanished from the board,
Queen Ebru appeared from nowhere,
Beautiful, young, wanting only to give,
And my antagonist complained,
"From where did *she* come?"
"You should know," I retorted,
"I am a yogi and the masters of yoga,
When they choose, remind me of their presence.
Nityananda, Muktananda, Babaji,
Mata Amritanandamayi,
Even Lord Krishna and Lord Jesus
May come to challenge *you*
When you challenge me."

The Waves

The waves asked the ocean,
"Why are you always
Hiding from us?"
The ocean went
Into a great stillness
And the waves found themselves
Without boundaries
And without complaints.

I Am a Lover of the Light

I am a lover of the light
A sunflower
Glowing in the sun
Turning to the east each morning
Bending to the west
When the hours
Run into darkness; then I sleep
And stay within
My inner light
In peace until the coming day.

Two Views of After

I.

She travels on the thought.
The room is warm, the flames of the fireplace
Catch her eye.
He speaks to her, William Shakespeare, her hero.
"Welcome, welcome."

II.

Time stretches out,
The last moment becomes the first moment,
The last breath merges with the infant's cry,
All is stillness.

Here I Am

Here I am wanting to write about the final days,
When it's past time to have our wills made,
And all I can think about is my friend Ehud,
Spending his last year seeking any possible cure,
My brother Dolph searching out meaning in the Vedanta
And my sister-in-law Adila, Israeli and a sabra,
Counting her view of the garden from the hospital window
As a wondrous gift.

A Mystery

Within the whirlwind and the tornadoes,
The stunned citizens, their crumbled homes,
Fear at its coming,
Grief after its going,
There is something greater,
More joyous, concealed.

Find it if you can.

The Sixth Principle

After the salutation to the sun,
Anita sits in lotus posture,
A trim figure in a leotard.
I, in the easy position.

There are four principles, she declares.
The first is—there is only *one* power.
With many names, I interject.
Silence and stillness
Being two of them, she says.

It wants your highest good,
The second principle.
What else could it want, I ask.
She frowns and continues:

Work with that power,
Keep in touch with those who know it.
These are principles three and four.
Take them to heart.

Take them to heart?
That makes *five,* I point out.
She gives me a quick look.
Let there be five principles,
Take them *all* to heart.

The lesson over, the meditation begins,
And I wonder what the *sixth* principle might be.
Focus on your breath, whispers Anita,
Focus on your breath.

The Guru's Touch

With this touch the body may vibrate,
No need to be concerned
If your torso shifts right to left
And your neck left to right.
You may find yourself straight upright
But standing on your head,
An ancient yogic posture.
No need to be concerned
If you feel fingers in your eyes
Rolling your eyeballs—
Trust the one in charge.

Satan, Prince of Darkness

(after Alexandra Devon)

Satan, Prince of Darkness,
Sorry to bother you
But I can't agree with your ways.
You say you are a counterforce,
An everlasting no that gets us going,
The challenge that yields strength and character.

It may be true that there is no drama,
No art, no progress, no interest even
Without you.
But I say *no* to your no,
Without giving reasons, freely,
Because I can and do.

Elusive

I love Anita who tells me
She is not a person
But an idea in the mind of God,
Which is fine by me,
Because the moment she slights me,
Scorns me or ignores me,
I will hate Anita-the-person
That she is
Not.

A Momentary Illusion

I was confused. I was astonished.
It was Ann Sheridan standing beside me,
Out of the cinematic past,
Out of my adolescence,
Statuesque and stately,
As we spoke to Sandy
In his hospital bed.
What are you doing here, Ann,
I wanted to say,
Shouldn't you be with Bogart or Cagney
Or with John Garfield,
Who will romantically put a cigarette between your lips?
Or have you become a yogini, Ann?
Are you now a spiritual guide?
And then I saw it was Anita, not Ann,
Anita, with her elusive smile,
Casting a spell on mortal mind.

The Real Ann Sheridan

"For me you are the real Ann Sheridan,"
This I confided to Anita,
 "Resurrected from my movie-going past,
The idol and ideal of my adolescent dreams."
"How is that," she asked, "Was Ann
Interested in the higher knowledge?"
"No, she was tough and down-to-earth."
"Did she practice yoga and meditation?"
"Never, that I heard of."
"Did she have compassion for all God's children?"
"That was not her forté."
Anita peered at me.
"Then how can I be like Ann Sheridan?"
"Simple," I explained, "the *real* Ann Sheridan
Is not at all like Ann Sheridan.
She is tender-hearted, with a loving spirit.
Just like you. You are *that* Ann Sheridan.
I speak from my truth."
"From your desire," was her only comment.

My Experience with a Famous Detective

The mystery arose for me
Almost overnight.
I called Wellington G. Wellington,
The famous London attorney and detective.
She insists she is my granddaughter.
She is twenty-eight and beautiful.
Her family is from Turkey and Macedonia
And I have never had sons or daughters.
Can you solve the paradox?
A week later Wellington G. Wellington
Returned my call. Unknown to me
He had entered his religious phase
And was deep in Bible study.
Simplicity, itself, he said.
All things are possible with God
And this one event is therefore
One of the things possible.
The pendulum turns this way and that,
The roulette wheel falls on the red and the black.
It is your turn to be a grandpa
And you may become a great-grandpa as well.
Faith is the key and
I will send you my bill in the mail.

Riddle

Between living and dreaming there is a third thing.
Antonio Machado

This is a riddle:
If I am her grandfather,
How can she be my mother?
Her name is Ebru—
And it is true—
But only in the space
Between living and dreaming.

Ruminations on a Bug

An elusive black bug,
Swifter than my swift-footed stomp,
Skittering along the bathroom wall,
Challenges me in two ways:
First, I ask myself,
Where is your reverence for life,
Your *ahimsa* now?
No answer but a different question
From a different corner.
How can you let a brainless insect
Outmaneuver and outwit you—
And in your own home?
Here, biology comes to assist me:
You and this bug are cousins,
With common ancestors and common DNA.
You are, so to speak, blood relatives—
It's a family affair!
I give thanks, then, to the world of science,
Which gives an answer
While it deepens the mystery.

The Aging Moment

It's here.
No, it's not here.
Gone, and gone again.
Can you grasp it?
Another one!
Where did it disappear to?
To memory! It's in memory now—
That image-making machine—
Years, so it says, of constructions
And deconstructions.
A liar from the beginning.

Anita Tests Me

> so much depends
> upon
>
> a red wheel
> barrow…
>> William Carlos Williams

Is the red wheelbarrow
A *red* wheelbarrow
If you're color-blind and see it green
Or is it
A *green* wheelbarrow?
A puzzling question, I reply.

Is the red color
In the wheelbarrow,
In the eye,
In the mind,
Or in the brain?

A difficult choice, I concede.

Is the mind in the brain
Or the brain in the mind
Or is the mind in the brain
Which is in the mind?
A conundrum, I say.

You've done very well, Anita tells me.
None of your answers can be disputed.

Reflection on What Ain't

By the way
I haven't seen an ice-box
In quite a while,
And the dumbwaiter that brought
The ice up to the kitchen
Can't be found.
Gone, gone, gone
Is the word *ain't.*
Say it ain't so, I say,
But soon
All that and all that
Will be gone,
Forgotten—
A mood,
A sense of things,
A life.

A Father's Story

What was the reason he sat me on his lap
To tell me the story of Julius Caesar?
Today I give thanks to my dad,
Who worked at machines all day—
Breathing in dust and grime,
A constant clatter in his ears,
In the midst of which came these words:
"Et tu Bruté?"
How did it happen he had memorized
Those speeches of Brutus and Mark Anthony ?
And then chose to remember them for me.
Shakespeare's creation
Alive again
In that moment
And this.

Past and Future

I'm from the street trolleys
With their overhead sparks,
Father buying corned beef and pastrami,
Pickles and potato salad
And, special for me,
Seltzer water with chocolate syrup.

I'm from Coney Island on Sundays
During the hot summers,
The crowded subway cars,
With everyone happy, both going
And coming back, at end of day
The arcades, the roller-coaster ride,
Dolph and I bumping each other
In our own little autos.

And where shall I be going?
Will my father buy me a special drink?
Will my brother say Hi?

The Open Door

It was the darkest place in the world.
Down the ramp, sweating, after our games,
Through a back door, sun left behind,
Then the passage going by an open cellar door,
The walls barely visible, then out into courtyard light.
Behind that cellar door what stood waiting?
A maniacal killer, an evil snatcher of children?
How often did I make that run
To get to the light.

Sonia, First Love

The name fills me with pleasure.
She on that bed, smiling and content,
Sitting in the middle of an ocean.
Near her
I am crawling about.
A strange bed, a strange room.
Kitchen odors give me joy.
Her mother suddenly
Appears with pudding.

I loved you, Sonia, for your radiant presence,
I love you now
For the memory of it.

A Boy's View of Mr. Moto Filtered
Through the Mind of an 81-Year-Old Man

Think fast, Mr. Moto,
Your back's against the wall,
Your enemies are closing in,
You're heading for a fall.

They've got you where they want you—
So they think, the fools,
You're much too quick, you've one more trick
And you never follow rules.

They come at you with clubs and knives
To meet your cool disdain
And then they fly above your head
Straight through the window pane.

For you're a master of the martial arts,
Respecter of the Tao,
A winner in the game of life
By living in the Now.

Zayde (Grandfather)

The lips that touched mine in childhood
Were not many, only my grandfather
Kissed me on the lips and he did so
Whenever we would meet, his beard
Brushing against my cheek and his whiskers
Entering my mouth every time.
We did not often visit the man
Whom my mother said drove her from her home.
We'd find him seated at a table
With books such as I had never seen before,
Monumental in my eyes,
Larger than I was, holy books that were
Buried with him when he died.
I would run to where he sat and the smile
He smiled before and after our caress
Gave me pleasure and made me smile too.
His wife, the wicked stepmother in my mother's story,
Was always out of sight,
But once I saw her son with a yarmulke on his head
And a prayer book in his hand.

My uncle Louie, too, was banished from their home,
My mother said, for reading an English-language periodical.
Though from another source, my cousin Joan,
I heard a somewhat different account:
Told that God would punish him,
Louie held up a dollar bill before his father's eyes,
Shouting his independence: "This... is my God."

The god of the dollar bill deserted my uncle
In the last years of the Great Depression.
With sons of his own and a wife that harped
On his weaknesses
And no work in sight,
Louie, despairing, swallowed a poison.
He lingered for weeks in a hospital,
Expressing remorse to all who visited
And died of pneumonia.
My grandfather left three years later,
Honored by his congregation,
Buried with the books he loved.

When I think of this family from time to time,
They seem like characters in a play just
Beyond the reach of reason.
I sense their irreconcilable conflict
And wish to say "be at peace with one another."
Yet I remember those kisses of my grandfather,
His beard against my cheek,
His whiskers on my tongue,
And the words of a child may come to the lips
That touched his lips,
"Thank you, Zayde. I love you still."

Invitation

It's time to come,
Oh dearest friend.
The rooms are in
Disorder, the bed
Unmade, the dishes
In the sink, I've
Lost the broom.

When I Become a Poet

When I become a poet,
The sky turns crimson
And the ginkgo tree laughs.

When I become a poet,
The more I disappear,
The more my truth appears.

When I become a poet,
Night cannot hold me,
The stars shine in daylight.

O Captain! My Captain!
The Missing Last Stanza

Fallen, cold and dead.
Walt Whitman

O captain, my captain I dreamt of you last night.
I saw you with the holy ones, the angels and
     the light.
And when you turned and spoke to me
     those words of tender care
I banished all my sorrow,
     I surrendered my despair.
Your love alone I witnessed – and life
     was everywhere!

A Poem of Praise

When the wheel turns
And the moment is right
A magical being
Can come
Unexpected
Show you a power
Of which you were barely aware
That can turn common to rare
Bare words into treasure
To open the heart
To widen the spirit.

And it was so
When Michelle came with her gifts.

The World's a Stage

We are such stuff as dreams are made on…
William Shakespeare

If my true self is perfect, as the holy ones teach,
And our life in time an illusion
Like a movie or a dream,
Then why, I asked Anita,
Do I have to do spiritual practices?
Or try to be considerate? Or honest?
Or anything?

The person who asks such a question, she said,
Is like Hamlet, the Prince of Denmark,
On the stage of a large theater,
Wondering whether to end his stepfather's life.
I assure you, Lawrence Olivier
Was not concerned about his stepfather—
For he had none—
Except when he became Hamlet
And then he understood it was a role
In a play
With great applause at the end
If he did it well.

Lawrence Olivier, I complained,
I don't see what Lawrence Olivier
Has to do with any of this.
But Anita was already responding:
Because you never see yourself as a role
In a play of your own creation,
Blending actor and role and playwright
In all you think and do.
The moment you have *this* understanding
Your acting will be impeccable,
Your knowledge complete,
And all heaven will applaud you as the curtain falls.

This is too fantastical for me, I objected.
Next you'll be telling me
I'm the heavenly audience that's applauding.

Right you are, were her departing words,
And who else should enjoy that divine artistry
That is your very own being?

A Thought on Reaching Ninety

Youth is wasted on the young,
Said a famous English playwright.
I say age is wasted on the aged,
Worrying about the ground
Being taken from under one's feet—
And the continual shock of losses—
Unless and until
We choose to be age-less
And learn the difficult art
Of walking on air.

Thank You

To Michelle de Savigny for ten years of guidance and inspiration and for the practical help required in creating a publishable manuscript.

To Ebru Kilinc and husband Ali for the generosity and love that led to the Ebru poems.

To Anita Koffler for her unfailing friendship and wisdom.

To Marjorie Holcombe, who first suggested the idea of a book and encouraged its completion.

To Lese Dunton, editor and publisher of the online publication *The New Sun* where four of my poems first appeared.

To Hamilton Senior Center for maintaining its poetry workshop through the years and to Chocolate Waters for her present leadership.

To all my family members and friends, whose support and encouragement through 90 years of living have been foundational.

About the Author

Irwin J. Goldman is a lifelong New Yorker. He was born in 1930, educated at Princeton and Columbia University, and worked professionally as a social psychologist. In 1980 he met the yogi and spiritual guide, Baba Muktananda, and has since pursued a spiritual way of life. The poems in this book were written after his becoming an octogenarian, with the understanding, "if you really want to know me, read my poems."

Back cover portrait of the author by David Ray.